Download music for I AM PERFECT for free from www.lubybuby.com

I AM PERFECT

written by Lubna Kharusi

illustrated by Amir and Meliha Al-Zubi

Music by Rene Gomez Sanchez, Thanae Pachiyannakis and Lubna Kharusi

lubybuby©

WORDS AND IDEAS THAT CAN CHANGE THE WORLD

www.lubybuby.com

Published by
Lubybuby 483 Green Lanes,
London, N13 4BS, UK,
www.lubybuby.com

ISBN 978-0-9930901-3-4

I AM PERFECT

MY NOSE MAY BE BIG,
I HAVE A SCARY GRIN,
YOU MAY EVEN JUDGE THE COLOR OF MY SKIN.

BUT THAT DOESN'T MATTER
I JUST LIFT UP MY CHIN,
'CAUSE I KNOW INSIDE I HAVE IT IN ME TO WIN.

IF YOU ONLY KNEW HOW PERFECT I AM,
IF YOU ONLY SAW ME FOR
WHO I REALLY AM.

YOU WOULD SEE MY POTENTIAL
TO SPREAD LOVE ON THIS EARTH.
IT IS WHY I AM HERE,
IT'S THE REASON FOR MY BIRTH.

HURTFUL WORDS DON'T CHANGE WHO I AM.
WHEN I FEEL PAIN, I KNOW THAT I CAN
FOCUS INSTEAD ON MY LOVE INSIDE.

KNOWING THERE IS NO NEED TO CRY OR HIDE,
BECAUSE I AM PERFECT,
THIS IS WHY I AM ALIVE.

IF I REALLY KNEW HOW PERFECT I AM,
I WOULD ONLY SEE MYSELF FOR
WHO I REALLY AM.

I WOULD KNOW MY POTENTIAL
TO SPREAD LOVE ON THIS EARTH.
IT IS WHY I AM HERE,
IT'S THE REASON FOR MY BIRTH.

PEOPLE KEEP TELLING ME HOW I SHOULD LIVE,
NO MATTER WHAT I DO,
OR HOW MUCH I GIVE.

NO NEED TO FEEL GUILTY,
NO NEED TO FEEL SHAME,
JUST BECAUSE OTHERS WANT SOMEONE ELSE
TO BLAME.

I BELIEVE AND KNOW HOW PERFECT I AM.
I TRUST AND SEE MYSELF FOR
WHO I REALLY AM.

I KNOW MY POTENTIAL,
TO SPREAD LOVE ON THIS EARTH.
IT IS WHY I AM HERE,
IT'S THE REASON FOR MY BIRTH.

EVEN IF YOU DON'T WANT TO PLAY WITH ME,
THE TRUE LOVE IN YOU IS
WHAT I SEE.

IN THIS MOMENT YOU MAY FEEL ANGRY, BUT BEHIND THAT ANGER I SEE PURE LOVE, JOY AND GLEE.

I RECOGNIZE IN YOU HOW PERFECT YOU ARE,
AND ONLY SEE YOU FOR
WHO YOU REALLY ARE.

I CAN SEE YOUR POTENTIAL TO SPREAD
LOVE ON THIS EARTH,
IT IS WHY YOU ARE HERE,
IT'S THE REASON FOR YOUR BIRTH.

WHETHER A BIRD, A HUMAN OR A KANGAROO,
WE ARE ALL HERE TO LOVE,
AND THAT IS WHAT'S TRUE.

CREATING A DIVIDE BETWEEN THE HUMAN RACE IS LIKE LOOKING IN THE MIRROR AND DENYING IT'S YOUR FACE.

LET US RECOGNIZE NOW, HOW PERFECT WE ARE!
AND ONLY SEE OURSELVES FOR
WHO WE REALLY ARE.

WE CAN REALIZE OUR POTENTIAL,
TO SPREAD LOVE ON THIS EARTH.
IT IS WHY WE ARE HERE,
IT'S THE REASON FOR OUR BIRTH.

TOGETHER WE CAN CHANGE
THIS PLANET OF OURS,
BY SHOWING LOVE TO ALL NEAR OR FAR.

WE CAN FEED ALL THE POOR,
WE CAN STOP ALL THE WARS,
WE CAN ENCOURAGE EACH OTHER
AND OPEN UP THE DOORS.

LET US LIVE THE PERFECTION THAT WE ARE,
AND UNCOVER OURSELVES
TO SHINE LIKE A STAR.

OUR POTENTIAL NEVER STOPS,
TO SPREAD LOVE ON THIS EARTH.
IT IS WHY WE ARE HERE,
IT'S THE REASON FOR OUR BIRTH.

DO FOR ANOTHER WHAT YOU
WANT FOR YOURSELF,
HELP THE SICK, AND BRING THEM TO HEALTH
HELP THE POOR, AND SPREAD YOUR WEALTH

SHARE YOUR LOVE,
AND LIVE YOUR PERFECT SELF.

LET US START TODAY!
WHAT ARE YOU GOING TO DO?
TO BRING OUT THE PERFECTION IN OTHERS
AND IN YOU?

MAKE A LIST, MAKE A PLAN
HAVE A VISION, TAKE A STAND
PEACE IS WITHIN ALL OF OUR HANDS.

Purchase our other
AMAZING BOOKS!
Download free Music & Videos from www.lubybuby.com
Lubna Kharusi
I LOVE YOU MORE THAN...
Picture Dictionary
ILLUSTRATIONS BY Amir AND Meliha Al-Zubi
FLY MY LITTLE BUTTERFLY
Lubna Kharusi
Amir Meliha Al-Zubi
Made of Love
by Lubna Kharusi
Amir Meliha Al-Zubi
Hakely Nakao Chavez, Thanae Pachiyannakis
Lubna Kharusi

www.ingramcontent.com/pod-product-compliance
Ingram Content Group UK Ltd.
Pitfield, Milton Keynes, MK11 3LW, UK
UKHW061950290726
14090UKWH00021B/1162

9 780993 090134